INSIDE THE NBA

# MINNESOTA TIMBERWOLVES

BY BRIAN HOWELL

SportsZone

An Imprint of Abdo Publishing
abdobooks.com

**abdobooks.com**

Published by Abdo Publishing, a division of ABDO, PO Box 398166, Minneapolis, Minnesota 55439. Copyright © 2023 by Abdo Consulting Group, Inc. International copyrights reserved in all countries. No part of this book may be reproduced in any form without written permission from the publisher. SportsZone™ is a trademark and logo of Abdo Publishing.

Printed in China.
052022
092022

Cover Photo: Mitchell Leff/Getty Images Sport/Getty Images
Interior Photos: Melinda Nagy/Shutterstock Images, 1; Thearon W. Henderson/Getty Images Sport/Getty Images, 4; Elsa/Getty Images Sport/Getty Images, 6, 20; Noah K. Murray/AP Images, 8; Harrison Barden/Getty Images Sport/Getty Images, 9; Steph Chambers/Getty Images Sport/Getty Images, 11; Ken Levine/Allsport/Getty Images Sport/Getty Images, 12; Focus on Sport/Getty Images Sport/Getty Images, 14; Ann Heisenfelt/AP Images, 16; Tom Strattman/AP Images, 18; Mark J. Terrill/AP Images, 23; Todd Warshaw/Allsport/Hulton Archive/Getty Images, 24; Harry How/Allsport/Getty Images Sport/Getty Images, 27; Jerry Holt/Star Tribune/Getty Images, 29; David Zalubowski/AP Images, 31; Ronald Martinez/Getty Images Sport/Getty Images, 33; Al Bello/Allsport/Getty Images Sport/Getty Images, 34; The Sporting News/Getty Images, 37; Rich Pedroncelli/AP Images, 38, 39; Hannah Foslien/Getty Images Sport/Getty Images, 41

Editor: Charlie Beattie
Series Designer: Joshua Olson

**Library of Congress Control Number: 2021952318**

**Publisher's Cataloging-in-Publication Data**

Names: Howell, Brian, author.
Title: Minnesota Timberwolves / by Brian Howell
Description: Minneapolis, Minnesota : Abdo Publishing, 2023 | Series: Inside the NBA | Includes online resources and index.
Identifiers: ISBN 9781532198359 (lib. bdg.) | ISBN 9781098272005 (ebook)
Subjects: LCSH: Minnesota Timberwolves (Basketball team)--Juvenile literature. | Basketball--Juvenile literature. | Professional sports--Juvenile literature. | Sports franchises--Juvenile literature.
Classification: DDC 796.32364--dc23

# TABLE OF
# CONTENTS

GOT-PAIN

# CHAPTER ONE

# YOUNG STARS ALIGN

**K**arl-Anthony Towns was in the clear. Seconds earlier the Minnesota Timberwolves center swatted the ball away from Phoenix Suns center Deandre Ayton. As Towns looked up, the path to the basket was open. He took two dribbles and brought the ball behind his head as he leaped toward the basket. Then he slammed down a thundering one-handed dunk.

On the surface, it was just another breakaway slam. Those plays happen all the time. Still early in the game, Towns's dunk put the Timberwolves up just 11–10. There was no crowd reaction. That's because, due to the COVID-19 pandemic, the stands at Phoenix Suns Arena were empty. However, the play was a taste of what was to come that night. And Towns was not alone. Two young Timberwolves were putting on a show.

Not much was expected of the Timberwolves as they entered the arena in Phoenix on March 18, 2021. The team

**Karl-Anthony Towns (32) averaged over 20 points per game for the fifth straight season in 2020–21.**

had made the playoffs just once in the previous 16 seasons. Minnesota's record was an NBA-worst 9–31. Just one month before, the Timberwolves had fired head coach Ryan Saunders. New coach Chris Finch was in his tenth game in charge. The Suns, on the other hand, were one of the best teams in the NBA.

However, the Timberwolves brought two incredible talents with them. The 25-year-old Towns had been the top pick in the 2015 NBA Draft. In six seasons he had emerged as one of the NBA's most dynamic big men. With the top pick in the 2020 draft, Minnesota gave him a running mate. Rookie guard Anthony Edwards was still learning the NBA game. But on any given night, he could be electric.

**Towns, *right*, starred at the University of Kentucky before the Timberwolves made him the number one overall pick in 2015.**

# HOT STARTS

With just over four minutes left in the first quarter, Edwards got a chance to show the Suns what he could do. The 19-year-old guard took a pass on the left wing. After a quick pump fake, he drove around a screen set by Towns. Edwards had a clear path to the basket, but Phoenix forward Jae Crowder was coming over to cut him off. As he approached the basket, Edwards quickly juked to his left. Crowder went flying past. All alone, Edwards threw down a two-handed dunk.

After the first quarter, the struggling Timberwolves were even with the mighty Suns. The score stood 25–25. Towns and Edwards had combined to score 19 points.

The second quarter belonged to the young Timberwolves guard. Early in the quarter, Edwards showed his outside range by hitting a tough, step-back three-pointer over Suns star Devin Booker. Two possessions later, he pulled up from five feet behind the three-point line. His shot sailed

## Edwards Goes First

Holding the first choice in the 2020 draft, the Wolves had a tough decision. Anthony Edwards from the University of Georgia, University of Memphis center James Wiseman, and point guard LaMelo Ball, who was playing professionally in Australia, were all considered potential top choices. The Wolves went with Edwards. He averaged more than 19 points per game his rookie season.

through the hoop, and the Timberwolves led 33–32. The rookie was far from done. One minute later, he put a quick crossover move on Phoenix's Abdel Nader at the top of the key. As the Suns' defender flailed, Edwards steamed down the lane. The rookie let out a scream as he threw down another forceful dunk.

## ECLIPSING THE SUNS

The two young stars were carrying the Timberwolves. By the end of the third quarter, Edwards had 33 points and Towns had 30. But Minnesota was in a familiar position. Led by Booker, the Suns built a 15-point third-quarter lead. Phoenix still held a 99–90 edge with 8:45 left in the game.

Guard D'Angelo Russell came to Minnesota in a trade with the Golden State Warriors on February 6, 2020.

The Timberwolves turned it on. In a 90-second stretch late in the game, Minnesota's young, electric duo took over again.

**Towns made his third All-Star team in 2022.**

With 5:18 left, Towns held the ball at the high post. Then he drilled a pass to Edwards, who managed to lay the ball into the hoop while being fouled. The basket gave the young guard a new career high of 35 points. After he knocked down the free throw, the Timberwolves trailed just 107–104.

For a 6-foot-11-inch center, Towns has exceptional shooting range. The next time down the floor, Edwards fed Towns for his fourth three-pointer of the night to tie the game. Phoenix responded with a jumper from point guard Chris Paul. But Towns and Edwards went straight back to work. The center fed the rookie for another layup. Once again, Edwards was fouled and hit the free throw.

After Phoenix briefly took the lead back, the Timberwolves responded again. Towns set a screen for Edwards, then peeled away toward the three-point line. Edwards whipped a one-handed pass to the big man for another three-pointer. The clock showed 3:52 remaining. In the previous 1:26, Towns and Edwards each had six points and two assists. More importantly, the Wolves now led 113–111.

## THE SPARK

Minnesota never trailed again. The 123–119 final shocked the Suns. Edwards finished with 42 points. Towns added 41, along with 10 rebounds and eight assists. After the game, compliments flew around the locker room.

"It's kind of fun playing with KAT, not going to lie," Edwards said, using a common nickname for Towns. "It was extremely fun."

"It's coming together for him. It's a beautiful thing to watch and a beautiful thing to be a part of," Towns added, praising Edwards in return.

At 10–31, the Timberwolves still had the worst record in the NBA. But the victory helped spark a turnaround. The rest of the year Minnesota went 14–18. Edwards finished second in NBA Rookie of the Year voting. Combined with point

Towns, *left,* finished the 2020–21 season averaging 24.8 points per game, while Edwards, *right,* averaged 19.3.

guard D'Angelo Russell, Minnesota had three star players, all 25 years old or younger. After the Phoenix game, Finch knew the Timberwolves were on the right track. "We love Ant's fearlessness. He has the ability, and playing next to KAT, they've got a nice little combination going."

On that March night in Phoenix, the young Timberwolves proved they could play with anyone in the NBA. For a franchise that had been down so long, it was a sign of hope for the future.

# CHAPTER TWO

# HERE COME THE WOLVES

In the late 1980s, the NBA was looking to grow beyond its 23 teams. In 1987 that became a reality. The league granted teams to four new cities. The Charlotte Hornets and Miami Heat were scheduled to start playing in 1988–89. A year later the Minnesota Timberwolves and Orlando Magic were set to join the league. For Minnesota fans, it was a return to the NBA.

At one time, the NBA's best team played in Minneapolis. The Minneapolis Lakers were the league's first dynasty, in the late 1940s and early 1950s. They won five titles in six years from 1949 to 1954. But the team struggled to make money. In 1960 the Lakers moved to Los Angeles. Now, 30 years later, the NBA was coming back to the Twin Cities of Minneapolis and St. Paul.

The fans were ready. The Timberwolves did not have their own arena yet. Instead, they played in the Hubert H. Humphrey Metrodome, home to football's Vikings and baseball's Twins.

Forward Tony Campbell was the Timberwolves' leading scorer in each of the team's first three seasons.

**Point guard Pooh Richardson was the Timberwolves' first-ever draft pick.**

The stadium held huge crowds for basketball. On November 8, 1989, when the Timberwolves played their first home game, 35,427 people showed up.

Minnesota lost that game to the Chicago Bulls 96–84. Even with a 22–60 record the first season, the fans still came out. Minnesota's announced attendance was 49,551 for its final home game of the year. It was the fourth-largest crowd in NBA history. For the season, Minnesota attracted an NBA record of 1,072,572 spectators.

## NEW HOME, SAME RESULTS

Minnesota moved into its permanent home, Target Center, the following season. It held 19,356 fans, standard for an NBA arena, but it was still full most nights. Drawing crowds was not a problem for Minnesota in its early seasons. However, finding victories was. Target Center opened with a 98–85 win for the Timberwolves over the Dallas Mavericks. But Minnesota finished 29–53 in 1990–91.

The Timberwolves' roster needed a lot of work. The team didn't get much help in the expansion draft. The college draft hadn't been very fruitful either. The team's first-ever pick, guard Pooh Richardson, played well but lasted only three seasons in Minnesota before he was traded. Center Felton Spencer, the team's top pick in 1990, lasted just as long.

The Timberwolves made their first big pickup after the 1990–91 season. General manager Jack McCloskey had just built back-to-back NBA champions with the Detroit Pistons. Minnesota hoped he could do it again. The Timberwolves thought they had their man in the 1992 draft. Forward Christian Laettner was one of the best college players ever. He helped Duke University to four Final Fours and back-to-back national titles. Before he ever played in the NBA, he won a gold medal at the 1992 Olympics in Barcelona, Spain, with Team USA's "Dream Team."

However, even Laettner could not turn around the lowly Timberwolves. Neither could the team's 1993 first-rounder, talented but troubled guard Isaiah Rider. Through the 1994–95 season, the Timberwolves had won more than 22 games only once in five years.

Beyond just losing games, Minnesota was close to losing its team completely. Original owners Harvey Ratner and Marv

Christian Laettner goes up for a layup against the Phoenix Suns during a game in 1992.

Wolfenson were deeply in debt over the cost of Target Center. The best option, they believed, was to sell the team. The pair even found buyers, but there was a catch. The new group wanted to move the Timberwolves to New Orleans.

In the end, the NBA said no to the deal. Local businessman Glen Taylor stepped in and bought the team, keeping it in Minnesota.

# THE BREAKTHROUGH

Taylor had a big job ahead in turning the team around. He went local for his new team president, hiring former NBA forward Kevin McHale. The Hall of Famer had played for the great Boston Celtics teams of the 1980s. He was also from the northern Minnesota town of Hibbing and had played college basketball at the University of Minnesota.

McHale's first big decision came at the 1995 NBA Draft. The Timberwolves held the fifth pick. At the time, almost all the players in the draft had multiple years of experience in college. McHale decided to take a gamble on a player fresh from high school. Forward Kevin Garnett was 6 feet, 11 inches tall, but skinny. Still, his combination of size and athleticism made NBA teams take notice. The Timberwolves' turnaround started the day Garnett joined the team.

Garnett couldn't do it alone. The Timberwolves still won only 26 games his rookie season. But for the first time, the team looked as if it had a bright future. And that future looked even sunnier after the 1996 draft. McHale picked guard Ray Allen. The rookie was immediately traded to the Milwaukee Bucks for the fourth pick, point guard Stephon Marbury.

Behind Garnett, Marbury, and veteran forward Tom Gugliotta, Minnesota shot up the standings. Flip Saunders, McHale's college teammate, was hired as general manager in May 1995. McHale named him head coach that December.

**The Timberwolves found their first superstar in 1995 when they drafted forward Kevin Garnett fifth overall.**

The team made the playoffs with a 40–42 record in Saunders's first full season in 1996–97. The next year the Timberwolves finished 45–37, the team's first winning record. The Timberwolves won their first playoff game too, before falling in five games to the Seattle SuperSonics.

Suddenly the Timberwolves were on the rise. Garnett and Marbury were two of the hottest young stars in the league. Even better, they were good friends off the court.

However, the team was about to splinter. Gugliotta left before the 1998–99 season. It didn't seem to matter, as Garnett was locked into a six-year contract worth $126 million. The problem came when Marbury needed a new contract too. The young point guard thought he should be the highest-paid player on the team. He refused to sign a new contract with Minnesota. Halfway through the 1998–99 season, the Timberwolves had no choice but to trade the 22-year-old.

Garnett was still good enough to get Minnesota to the playoffs. But he couldn't deliver playoff success by himself. Despite winning 50 games three times, the team lost in the first round seven years in a row.

The team also made a huge blunder off the court. In 1999 McHale tried to sign forward Joe Smith. The deal was made, but the NBA said the Timberwolves broke the league's contract rules. McHale was suspended for an entire season. And the Timberwolves were stripped of five first-round picks. However, the league eventually gave two of the draft choices back.

## PLAYOFF BREAKTHROUGH

The 2003–04 Timberwolves had a new look. In the offseason, McHale made big moves to bring in veteran players around Garnett. Point guard Sam Cassell and small forward Latrell Sprewell provided offense. Role players like guards Trenton Hassell and Fred Hoiberg, along with center Michael Olowokandi filled out the roster.

Additions like veteran point guard Sam Cassell (19) helped the Timberwolves reach the Western Conference finals in 2004.

The combination paid off. At 58–24, Minnesota was the best team in the Western Conference. And it had the league MVP in Garnett. The Timberwolves finally won a playoff series, knocking off the Denver Nuggets in the first round. Then they advanced to the Western Conference finals by outlasting the powerful Sacramento Kings. In the conference finals, Minnesota faced the era's dominant team, the Los Angeles Lakers. The Timberwolves' magical run finally ended in a six-game series.

It looked as if the Timberwolves were set up for long-term success. Instead, it all came crashing down the next year. Saunders was fired midseason after a bad start. McHale took over for the rest of the year. Despite finishing 44–38, Minnesota missed the playoffs.

Over the next few seasons Minnesota sank back down the standings. Garnett was traded to the Boston Celtics in 2007. The team hoped to rebuild around some of the young players who arrived in that deal. Instead, it continued a playoff drought that stretched over a decade.

## YOUNG PUPS

The Timberwolves churned through players and coaches. Some players showed great promise. At times the team looked as if it might be figuring things out. But every season ended the same way. In 2014–15, even Saunders came back to give it another go as the team's coach. With a 16–66 record, Minnesota posted its eleventh straight losing season.

The Timberwolves had been the NBA's worst team before, but they had never gotten the top draft pick. That finally changed in the summer of 2015. With it, the Wolves picked University of Kentucky center Karl-Anthony Towns.

Towns, like Garnett before him, was a unique talent. As a big man, he could score at will all over the court. Along with young guard Zach LaVine and forward Andrew Wiggins, the Timberwolves finally were looking up again.

In 2016–17 Minnesota extended its streak of losing seasons to 13 in a row. Enough was enough. The team traded LaVine to the Chicago Bulls as part of a deal for Jimmy Butler. The veteran guard brought experience and intensity not often seen in Minnesota since Garnett left in 2007. With tough-minded coach Tom Thibodeau leading them, the Timberwolves finally posted a winning record and returned to the playoffs in 2018.

Once again the team looked as if it was on the rise. But again it came apart quickly. Butler grew upset the next season and asked to be traded. The Timberwolves faded back to their losing ways.

Fans started to see light at the end of the tunnel in 2020. The Timberwolves had the first pick in that year's draft and took high-scoring guard Anthony Edwards. After starting slowly his rookie year, Edwards posted 40 straight double-figure

**Timberwolves guard Anthony Edwards (1) made the NBA All-Rookie Team in 2020–21.**

scoring games to end the season. The next season, Edwards, Towns and point guard D'Angelo Russell formed a solid trio. The young Timberwolves improved dramatically. After finishing 46–36, the team brought both excitement and playoff basketball back to Minnesota.

# CHAPTER THREE

# LEADERS OF THE PACK

In 1995 general manager Flip Saunders and team president Kevin McHale needed to change the Timberwolves' losing ways. They decided to take a big risk at the draft.

At the time, high school players were allowed to jump straight to the NBA. But no one had done it in 20 years. Garnett had been a dominant player at a prep school in Chicago. He decided he was ready for the NBA and the payday that would come with it. The Timberwolves agreed.

The Wolves took Garnett fifth overall. At the time, he was the youngest player in NBA history. That didn't stop him from becoming a star. Garnett came off the bench early in his rookie season, then took over for veteran Sam Mitchell in the starting lineup. He finished fourth on the team in scoring, but Mitchell knew Garnett was going to be a star.

**Kevin Garnett was an All-Star 12 times in 14 seasons with the Timberwolves.**

"First day. Doug West, myself, we knew first day," Mitchell said. "I remember walking off the court, we looked at each other and said, 'One day, we're going to tell people we played with Kevin Garnett.'"

Garnett won the veterans over with his intensity and professionalism. He beat opponents because of his blend of size and skill. Garnett was listed at 6 feet, 11 inches tall. When Garnett came to the NBA, most players that size played only down low. Garnett's success is a big reason modern big men can shoot both inside and outside.

He also changed how players entered the league. After he went straight from high school to the pros, other teenagers followed. Kobe Bryant was drafted the year after Garnett. In 2001 three of the top four picks were high schoolers. While Garnett and Bryant turned into stars, many young players did not. The NBA had so many teenagers enter the league and fail that the league changed the rules. The NBA decided in 2005 that players had to be at least one year out of high school to join the league.

In his second year Garnett became a true NBA star. His rise helped the Timberwolves reach the playoffs for the first time. But the forward didn't do it alone.

Power forward Tom Gugliotta joined the Timberwolves halfway through the 1994–95 season. He was a vital scorer for Minnesota's first two playoff teams. When the Timberwolves

Forward Tom Gugliotta, *left*, averaged a career-high 20.6 points per game for Minnesota during the 1996–97 season.

made the postseason for the first time in 1996–97, Gugliotta led them in scoring. He also made his only career All-Star team that year.

Point guard Stephon Marbury was just 19 years old that season. But he stepped right into the Timberwolves lineup and averaged more than 15 points and seven assists per game. The flashy point guard from New York City brought extra style to the Timberwolves. He and Garnett made the league take notice of the young team. Several players around the league compared them to Karl Malone and John Stockton. That Hall of Fame pair had led the Utah Jazz to the playoffs for more than a decade.

Marbury lasted only two full seasons in Minnesota. He asked to leave in 1999 after the team refused to give him a contract bigger than Garnett's. Gugliotta had already left. He thought Marbury was a selfish player, so Gugliotta signed with the Phoenix Suns in 1998. By the time Garnett won the NBA MVP Award in 2004, he was the only one of the three stars left in Minnesota.

## THE COACH

When McHale needed some help building the Timberwolves in 1995, he turned to an old college friend. Saunders had been a point guard at the University of Minnesota. But he did not go on to an NBA playing career. Instead, he became a successful coach in basketball's minor leagues.

With the Timberwolves struggling in December 1995, McHale replaced head coach Bill Blair. He hired Saunders, who was already Minnesota's general manager. It proved to be a perfect fit. Saunders had a fatherly style that worked well for young players like Garnett.

**Coach Flip Saunders, *left*, had a winning record nine times in 11 seasons with the Timberwolves.**

Saunders turned the Timberwolves into a playoff team. He was still there to guide them to their best season ever in 2003–04, when they reached the Western Conference finals.

Saunders was fired during the 2004–05 season. But he returned nearly a decade later. In 2013 he was hired as the team president to try to stabilize the franchise that had floundered while he was gone. Less than a year later, Saunders took over coaching the Timberwolves again.

The team struggled during his one season on the bench. But Saunders received worse news that offseason. He was diagnosed with Hodgkin's lymphoma. Though he planned to come back and coach in 2015–16 after receiving treatment, he was never healthy enough. Saunders died on October 25, 2015. Two seasons later, at Target Center, the team raised a banner that read "Flip" to honor the late coach.

## LOVE IT

While Garnett remained one of the league's elite big men, the Timberwolves team around him struggled to keep up after their 2004 run. By 2007 the team was well out of contention and traded Garnett to the Boston Celtics. It was time for a new era in Minnesota.

### The Trio

A big reason for Minnesota's 2004 playoff run was the play of guard Sam Cassell and forward Latrell Sprewell complementing Kevin Garnett. Both joined the team in the summer of 2003. Cassell made his only All-Star team that year. Sprewell averaged nearly 20 points per game in the playoffs. The trio didn't last long, however. Both Sprewell and Cassell were gone from Minnesota after the 2004–05 season.

The players Minnesota got back in the Garnett trade never panned out as stars. However, the power forward they drafted one year later did. Kevin Love made the All-Rookie team his first year.

Like Garnett, he could play both inside and outside. Love grew into a 20-point scorer and led the NBA in rebounding during his third season with an average of 15.2 points per game. At one point in 2010–11, Love compiled double-doubles

Power forward Kevin Love made three All-Star teams in six seasons with the Timberwolves, and he was the NBA's top rebounder in 2010–11.

in 53 straight games. That was the longest streak in the NBA since 1980. The only thing missing was team success. The Timberwolves never had a winning season in Love's six years with the team. Even the addition of slick-passing point guard Ricky Rubio in 2011 did not help. The Spaniard averaged more than eight assists per game during two stints with the Timberwolves. But injuries often kept him off the court.

## TIME FOR TOWNS

Once again the Timberwolves had reached a dead end and were looking for answers. Before the 2014–15 season, they traded Love to the Cleveland Cavaliers. A year later, after another dismal season, the Timberwolves had the first pick in the 2015 draft. With it, they selected 6-foot-11-inch center Karl-Anthony Towns.

Towns had played for a star-studded team at the University of Kentucky. With so many skilled teammates, he didn't have to dominate in college. In the pros, he quickly showed he had the skills to be a top player. He was a double-double machine who could power his way to the basket and shoot from outside.

Towns helped Minnesota get back to the postseason in his third season. He had help from shooting guard Jimmy Butler. The pair gave Minnesota a dangerous inside-outside combo. When Butler came over in a trade from Chicago, he brought an intense attitude with him. The following season, his fiery personality clashed with what he thought was Towns's laid-back approach. The two players argued often. Butler also clashed with head coach Tom Thibodeau. The conflicts ended when Butler left the team in a trade to the Philadelphia 76ers.

When Butler left, the Timberwolves needed more help to get back to the postseason. They added scoring point guard D'Angelo Russell in a trade near the end of the 2019–20 season. In that year's draft, shooting guard Anthony Edwards came on board. Many fans thought Minnesota had its most talented trio since Garnett, Sam Cassell, and Latrell Sprewell. And they hoped this group would stay together long enough to experience playoff success.

Minnesota center Karl-Anthony Towns, *top*, was the NBA's Rookie of the Year in 2015–16.

# CHAPTER FOUR

# MINNESOTA MOMENTS

The NBA awarded the All-Star Game to Minnesota in 1994. The struggling Timberwolves didn't have any players in the game. But guard Isaiah "J. R." Rider still found a way to steal the show.

The shooting guard had been the team's first-round pick the summer before. On the day he was drafted, he guaranteed a win in the dunk contest. On February 12, 1994, he set out to back up his boast.

Rider showed off his leaping ability over multiple rounds. On his first dunk of the finals, Rider sprinted out of the corner and exploded toward the basket. He brought the ball down between his legs while jumping and powered it through the hoop. The crowd erupted. NBA legend Charles Barkley, working on the television broadcast, said it "might be the best dunk I've ever seen."

**Isaiah Rider averaged 18.8 points per game during his three seasons in Minnesota.**

The dunk was nicknamed "East Bay Funk" after Rider's hometown of Oakland, California. The signature slam scored 49 out of a possible 50 points. When the competition ended, he was the winner—just as he said he would be.

# POSTSEASON BOUND

Minnesota's first seven seasons proved to be one of the worst stretches for a team in NBA history. The team compiled a record of 152–422. Those losing ways started to change in 1996–97. At the end of the year, the Timberwolves were 40–42, just good enough to make the playoffs.

However, they weren't good enough to stay long. The favored Houston Rockets swept Minnesota in the best-of-five first round. Timberwolves fans waved white towels before Game 3 that read "Bring it on!" The Rockets did, defeating Minnesota 125–120.

The next year Minnesota faced the favored Seattle SuperSonics in the first round. It looked like another short stay after Seattle blew out Minnesota 108–83 in the first game.

But Minnesota bounced back. Garnett's layup with 3:02 left in Game 2 broke an 86–86 tie. Minnesota never trailed again in a 98–93 win.

The Timberwolves claimed their first playoff victory back home for Game 3. Seattle led by five at the start of the fourth quarter. The Timberwolves responded with a 26–6 run on their way to a 98–90 win in front of a raucous home crowd. The Sonics rebounded to win the series. But Minnesota looked like a young team on the rise.

## BREAKING THROUGH

**Stephon Marbury led the Timberwolves with 25 points and seven assists in the team's first playoff win on April 26, 1998.**

Minnesota continued reaching the playoffs each year, only to suffer first-round defeat. The team finally got over the hump in 2003–04.

Veterans Sam Cassell and Latrell Sprewell joined Garnett to give the Timberwolves their first "Big Three." And behind

Timberwolves small forward Latrell Sprewell celebrates the team's 114–113 overtime victory over the Sacramento Kings in Game 3 of the teams' 2004 playoff series.

Garnett's MVP season, Minnesota earned not only its first division title but also the top seed in the West. Suddenly, the Timberwolves had gone from underdogs to championship favorites.

The Timberwolves went up 3–1 in the best-of-seven opening series against the Denver Nuggets. Game 5 was back home. Garnett made sure that's where the series ended. His 28 points, seven rebounds, and eight assists led the team to a 102–91 win. After the long wait to win a playoff series, Garnett summed it up in his postgame interview. "This is for everybody," he said.

A tough Sacramento Kings team awaited in the second round. The series ultimately came down to a seventh game. The Timberwolves led 79–70 with 3:10 left, but they were struggling to hit shots. The Wolves did not hit a field goal the rest of the game. Minnesota point guard Sam Cassell knocked down two free throws with 16 seconds remaining to prevent total collapse. The shots put Minnesota up 83–80. The lead held up when the Kings missed two three-pointers on their final possession. Garnett was the star again, finishing with 32 points and 21 rebounds.

That set up a Western Conference finals showdown against the Lakers. The team that had won three straight championships from 2000 to 2002 already had two superstars in Kobe Bryant and Shaquille O'Neal. Before this season, it had added two more future Hall of Famers in Karl Malone and Gary Payton. The Lakers won three of the first four games.

**Kevin Garnett (21) goes up for a jump shot against the Kings during the 2004 playoffs.**

Despite a monster effort from Garnett in Game 5, when he posted 30 points and 19 rebounds, the Lakers held on to win in six games. Though it was a disappointing end, it was still the best season in Timberwolves history.

# 30 LOVE

Minnesota forward Kevin Love put together a 53-game streak of double-doubles during the 2010–11 season. However, his most impressive game that year came outside the streak. On November 12, 2010, the Timberwolves hosted the New York Knicks. The final score was 112–103 Minnesota. Love had his fingerprints all over the box score. He finished the night with 31 points, second only to Timberwolves small forward Michael Beasley. But Love also had 31 rebounds.

The forward sealed the deal in dramatic fashion. He drilled a three-pointer from the top of the key with 1:17 left for his final basket of the night. It was the first 30/30 game in the NBA since Hall of Fame center Moses Malone did it in 1982.

# BACK IN THE DANCE

The playoffs hadn't officially started when the Timberwolves hosted the Denver Nuggets on April 11, 2018. But they might as well have. Both teams entered the final day of the season 46–35. In the strong Western Conference, that meant neither had yet clinched a playoff berth. Only one spot remained. It was a winner-take-all game. The dramatic finale went to overtime. With 1:19 left, the Timberwolves trailed by one. Minnesota had the ball but was running out of time on the shot clock. Point guard Jeff Teague drove in from the left wing and threw up a one-handed floater. The ball dropped

Jimmy Butler (23) and Karl-Anthony Towns (32) celebrate the Timberwolves' victory over the Denver Nuggets on the final day of the 2017–18 season.

through, and Minnesota took the lead for good. The victory ended the Timberwolves' streak of 13 seasons without a playoff appearance. Stars Jimmy Butler and Karl-Anthony Towns led the way for Minnesota. Butler finished with 31 points. Towns had a double-double of 26 points and 14 rebounds.

A year later, Butler left the team. It was again the start of a new era in Minnesota. As the Timberwolves added new talent around Towns, they hoped for more nights like April 11, 2018.

# TIMELINE

## 1987

The NBA decides to add four teams. Miami and Charlotte join the league one year later. The Timberwolves and Orlando Magic are set to start in 1989.

## 1989

The Timberwolves begin their first NBA season on November 3. The team finishes 22–60 in its first year.

## 1990

A crowd of 49,551 fans turn out to see the Timberwolves' home finale against the Denver Nuggets. It is the fourth-largest crowd in NBA history.

## 1994

The team is sold to Minnesota businessman Glen Taylor.

## 1995

The team hires Kevin McHale as general manager. McHale hires Flip Saunders as head coach and drafts high schooler Kevin Garnett fifth overall in the 1995 draft.

## 1997

Led by All-Star forwards Garnett and Tom Gugliotta, as well as rookie point guard Stephon Marbury, the Timberwolves make the playoffs for the first time but lose to the Houston Rockets in a three-game sweep.

## 1998

Minnesota reaches the playoffs again and wins two games against the Seattle SuperSonics before falling in a five-game series.

## 2004

Led by league MVP Garnett, the Timberwolves win their first-ever playoff series by beating the Denver Nuggets in five games. Minnesota advances to the Western Conference finals with a seven-game victory over the Sacramento Kings in round two.

## 2007

Garnett is traded to the Boston Celtics after the Timberwolves finish 32–50.

## 2010

Minnesota forward Kevin Love records the first 30/30 NBA game in 28 years by posting 31 points and 31 rebounds in a 112–103 win over the New York Knicks.

## 2014

Love is traded to the Cleveland Cavaliers in August. Number one overall pick Andrew Wiggins arrives in Minnesota in the deal.

## 2015

The Timberwolves draft center Karl-Anthony Towns first overall.

## 2018

The Timberwolves defeat the Denver Nuggets 112–106 in overtime on the final day of the regular season to qualify for the playoffs for the first time in 14 years.

## 2020

The Wolves select guard Anthony Edwards with the number one overall pick in the NBA Draft.

## FRANCHISE HISTORY
Minnesota Timberwolves
(1989– )

## KEY PLAYERS
Tony Campbell (1989–92)
Sam Cassell (2003–05)
Anthony Edwards (2020– )
Kevin Garnett (1995–2007,
2015–16)
Tom Gugliotta (1995–98)
Kevin Love (2008–14)
Sam Mitchell (1989–92,
1995–2002)
Ricky Rubio (2011–17, 2020–21)
D'Angelo Russell (2020– )
Wally Szczerbiak (1999–2006)
Karl-Anthony Towns (2015– )
Andrew Wiggins (2014–20)

## KEY COACHES
Flip Saunders (1995–2005,
2014–15)
Tom Thibodeau (2016–19)

## HOME ARENAS
Hubert H. Humphrey
Metrodome (1989–90)
Target Center (1990– )

# TRIVIA

## BY POPULAR VOTE

Minnesota selected two finalists for its nickname when the team was founded, "Timberwolves" and "Polars." Minnesota's 842 city councils were each asked to vote. "Timberwolves" won by a 2-to-1 margin.

## A FAIR FOUL SHOOTER

Timberwolves guard Michael Williams set an NBA record with 97 consecutive made free throws in 1993. He made his last 84 of the 1992–93 season and then his first 13 of the 1993–94 season.

## GUESS WHO'S BACK

The first coach in Wolves history was Bill Musselman. He coached the team for its first two seasons. It was his second time coaching in the state, as he was the head coach of the University of Minnesota men's basketball team from 1971–75.

## HOW TALL ARE YOU?

While Kevin Garnett was listed at 6 feet, 11 inches, he might be taller. It was rumored he didn't want to be known as a 7-footer, because everyone would think he was a center. His former coach had a creative answer when asked how tall Garnett was. Flip Saunders used to tell interviewers that Garnett was "6-foot-13."

# GLOSSARY

**assist**
A pass that leads directly to a basket.

**berth**
A spot in a competition or tournament earned through previous results.

**draft**
A system that allows teams to acquire new players coming into a league.

**dynamic**
Energetic and exciting; in sports, usually referring to an athlete with one or more outstanding skills.

**expansion**
The addition of new teams to increase the size of a league.

**franchise**
A sports organization, including the top-level team and all minor league affiliates.

**overtime**
An extra period of play when the score is tied after regulation.

**postseason**
Another word for playoffs; the time after the end of the regular season when teams play to determine a champion.

**rebound**
To catch the ball after a shot has been missed.

**rookie**
A professional athlete in his or her first year of competition.

**roster**
A list of players who make up a team.

**screen**
When an offensive player legally blocks the path of a defender to open up a teammate for a shot or a pass.

**veteran**
A player who has played many years.

# MORE **INFORMATION**

## BOOKS

Flynn, Brendan. *The NBA Encyclopedia for Kids*. Minneapolis, MN: Abdo Publishing, 2022.

Mahoney, Brian. *GOATs of Basketball*. Minneapolis, MN: Abdo Publishing, 2022.

Ybarra, Andres. *Great Basketball Debates*. Minneapolis, MN: Abdo Publishing, 2019.

## ONLINE RESOURCES

To learn more about the Minnesota Timberwolves, please visit **abdobooklinks.com** or scan this QR code. These links are routinely monitored and updated to provide the most current information available.

# INDEX



## ABOUT THE AUTHOR

Brian Howell has been an author and sports journalist for more than 28 years. He has written several books about sports and covered major events such as the US Open golf tournament, the World Series, the Stanley Cup Playoffs, the NBA All-Star Game, and playoff games in the NBA and NFL. He has earned several writing awards during his career. The Colorado native lives with his wife and four children.